We
Dr. Lyn Is In

How to Break Up, Survive and Thrive

By Lyn Kelley, Ph.D., CPC
Certified Professional Coach

"My mission is to provide understanding, comfort, knowledge, wisdom and personal power in relationships."

Published by GROW Publications
Cover Art by www.caligraphics.com

What others are saying about Dr. Lyn's
Dear Jane Series

"This book saved me! I just had a horrible breakup with my boyfriend of 3 years and this book got me through it. It made me realize that sometimes the right thing to do is the hardest thing to do. I'm moving on with my life now!

It was a pleasure speaking with you earlier and look forward to our next conversation. Thank you so much for this book. I can hardly to start reading it. Your books are interesting and just grab your attention instantly."
--Sue Grady, Stanton, OH

"Dr. Kelley tells it like it is. I've read all of her books on relationships and feel I have grown by leaps and bounds due to her honest, straight, real information. She writes like she is talking to her best friend. All the strategies I've used so far that she suggests have worked for me! I feel so much more confident in dating now, and I'm not wasting time with men who are wrong for me. This was worth more than 100 times the cost of the books to me. I highly recommend her books."
--Tanya Murray, San Diego, CA

"Best Book Ever! Lyn Kelly is the best author. I have read at least 5 of her books. Best one - Bad Dick Good Jane. Her advice is rock solid. Will enlighten you and open your eyes to the truth. I am a true fan. You won't be disappointed."
--Ashton, Amazon.com Review

"I am still currently in "Dating Detox." I really loved this book. It was motivating and inspiring. I feel I can really get through this tough time and "Survive and Thrive!!" Thank you Lyn!!"
--Sarah, Amazon.com Review

"I have read two of your books; The 12 Biggest Mistakes and How to Cure a Commitment Phobic. Both were brilliant and really well written. I really enjoyed them and will recommend them to my friends for sure."
--Michelle, Worcestershire, UK

"Lyn Kelley has done a superlative job of explaining why people fail at their relationships and how they can stop this self-sabotage. She explains how to know which men are 'manageable' and which men are not. She gives concrete, simple ways to get even the most difficult men to surrender to you. She showed me how I was actually pushing men away from me rather than moving them toward me. I now know what I've been doing wrong and am committed to changing myself! I highly recommend this book."
--**Michelle Rodriguez, Orlando, FL**

"Dear Dr. Lyn,
I just wanted to let you know how amazing and accurate your book is (10 Secrets to Getting Any Man You Want to Want YOU). This book answered all of my questions and I realized what I was doing wrong. Forget women are from Venus and blah blah blah. YOUR BOOK SAYS IT ALL! Thank you."
--Katie Rox

How to Break Up, Survive and Thrive

By Lyn Kelley, Ph.D., CPC
Certified Professional Coach

Copyright 2018 GROW Publications

Dear Jane Series:
Book 1: *The 12 Biggest Mistakes Women Make in Dating & Love Relationships*
Book 2: *How to Cure a Commitment-Phobic*
Book 3: *How to Turn a Player into a Stayer*
Book 4: *Controlling and Manipulative Men: How to Spot Them and Handle Them*
Book 5: *Self-Centered and Narcissistic Men: How to Spot Them and Handle Them*
Book 6: *Addicted Men – Drugs, Alcohol, Porn and More: How to Spot Them and Handle Them*
Book 7: *Low Achieving Men - Passives, Wimps, Dreamers: How to Spot Them and Handle Them*
Book 8: *Cheap Men: How to Spot Them and Handle Them*
Book 9: *Men who Lie and Cheat: How to Spot Them and Handle Them*
Book 10: *Emotionally Unavailable Men: How to Spot Them and Handle Them*
Book 11: *The Romantic Terrorist: Protect Yourself from Stalking, Harassment, Bullying and Threats*
Book 12: *How to Get Any Man You Want to Want YOU*
Book 13: *The 10 Biggest Mistakes Men Make in Dating & Love Relationships*
Book 14: *How to Break Up, Survive and Thrive*
Book 15: *Bad Dick, Good Jane: How Good Girls Get Bad Boys to Behave, Fall in Love and Commit*

New Release!
*Bad Dick, Good Jane:
How Good Girls Get Bad Boys to Behave, Fall in Love, and Commit*

Other Self-Help Books by Lyn Kelley:
How to Stick With Your Diet & Exercise Program
Light their Fire: Right and Wrong Ways to Coach and Motivate People
The 7 Self-Sabotages: Why People Sabotage Themselves and How to Stop It
How to Become Your Own Life Coach in 12 Easy Steps
Stalking 101: Everything You Need to Know to Keep Yourself Safe
How to Motivate Yourself: Secrets of the Motivational Superstars
The Magic of Detachment: How to Detach from Other People and Their Problems
One Day She Woke Up and Decided to Be Brave

I offer telephone and email coaching. Contact me to set up an appointment!

lyn@janesgoodadvice.com

Learn more about Dr. Lyn and Relationship Coaching and sign up for her FREE *Dear Jane Advice Column* at www.janesgoodadvice.com

Follow Dr. Lyn:
Facebook: http://facebook.com/ lyn.kelley1
Twitter: http://wefollow.com/JanesGoodAdvice
LinkedIn: http://www.linkedin.com/in/drlynisin

See Dr. Lyn's YouTube videos:
The Biggest Mistake Women Make in Dating and Love Relationships:
http://youtu.be/--aGjh3WgPc

Is He a Commitment Phobic?
http://www.youtube.com/watch?v=cLCqQHzmNOA

How to Stick With Your Diet and Exercise Program:
http://youtu.be/SEJvHJkKtSM

How to Break Up, Survive and Thrive
By Lyn Kelley, Ph.D., CPC

Table of Contents

Introduction

Chapter 1: Normal Stages of a Relationship

Honeymoon
Disillusionment
Conflict and Negotiation
Plateau
Commitment

Chapter 2: When the Dream Dies

Fairy Tales
Expectations

Chapter 3: How to Know If You Should Break Up

Your Five Guiding Forces
The 9 Worst and the 9 Best Character Traits for a Good Relationship
The 3 A's
Ambivalence
Should We Just Take a Break?
What If He's a Great Guy But I'm Just Not That IN to Him?

Chapter 4: How to Do It When You Are the One to End It

How to End It When You're Just Not That IN to Him
How to End It When He's Not Right (or Good) For You
Can We Remain Friends?
Personal Boundaries

When to Amputate
You Don't Know a Man Until You Break Up With Him

Chapter 5: How to Handle It When Your Mate Is the One to End It

He Breaks Up With You But Can't Let You Go
The Addictive Relationship

Chapter 6: The Yo-Yo Syndrome

On Again, Off Again
Tough Love
Drop the Need for Revenge
The 7 Worst Things You Can Do
The 7 Ways to Move On

Chapter 7: Healthy Grieving

Denial
Anger
Bargaining
Sadness, Disappointment, Depression
How to Get Through the Pain
Acceptance
Healing
Reintegration

Chapter 8: How to Get Over It

Can Chemistry Be Changed?
Stop the Insanity!
Dating Detox
New Commitments

Chapter 9: Moving On and Thriving

Self Focus
What Oprah Knows For Sure

Chapter 10: Comes the Dawn

Let It Go
Comes the Dawn

Introduction

Let's face it, breaking up is hard. It doesn't matter if you're the one doing it or your mate is the one doing it, it's painful either way. I've been through more than my fair share of breakups, and there's just no easy way to do it. That being said, the *easiest* way is when it's the *right* time and the *right* way. When you know it's *right* to break it off with your lover, you can get through the pain of loss. If you do it in the *right* way, it will be much easier.

This book is for those who are currently in relationships that they know are not right for them. It is also for those who are in a relationship that they aren't sure is right for them. It is also for people who have just ended a relationship, or are separated temporarily. It is for anyone in a difficult relationship of any kind who is struggling with whether or not to end it. I write in terms of women and men in love relationships, however <u>these ideas can be applied to any relationship, male or female, gay or straight, family member, co-worker, boss, employee, business partner, friend, etc</u>. Since the English language doesn't have an appropriate pronoun for all of the above, I write this from the female perspective, in a relationship with a man, but you can simply change the words to fit your situation.

If you are feeling frustrated, distressed or sad due to problems in your relationship, it is often difficult to judge the situation clearly. You may feel you love your mate strongly and if you end the relationship your life will be empty and lonely. You may feel that even though your relationship is not perfect you still want to hold on to it, since you believe you might never find another person who you can love as strongly as you think you love your mate. Or you may be fearful you'll never find a mate who loves you as strongly as your mate does. You may feel guilty for wanting to end it. You may be worried that your mate will not be able to handle it emotionally, and may become a danger to himself or others. You may know you don't really want him but you don't want anyone else to have him! There are so many obstacles in your mind, you don't know what to do. So you become a prisoner of this relationship. You live behind invisible bars that your confused emotions have created.

It may have become so bad that you feel like a P.O.W. You are a prisoner of war. You may be a victim of abuse – emotional, mental or physical. You may be being mistreated, degraded, demeaned, betrayed, and beat down. Even if your mate is good to you, you may still suffer from the emotional turmoil of guilt and shame. Or you may be bound by knowing you need to leave but don't know how, and don't have the strength or the resources.

Throughout this book I will refer to women as "Good Janes" or "Bad Janes." This is because I spent seven years writing a book called ***Bad Dick, Good Jane: How Good Girls Get Bad Boys to Behave, Fall in Love and Commit***. There are three main types of "Janes." "Plain Jane" is compliant, nice, quiet and codependent. "G.I. Jane" is the fighter, bitch, drama queen, and emotional wreck. "Good Jane" is confident, empowered, strong, rational and clear about what she wants and doesn't want. I want you to know how to be a "Good Jane" even when you're breaking up with a guy. There are right and wrong ways to do it!

In this book (***Bad Dick, Good Jane***) I describe the nine worst kinds of men for relationships. Most "Bad Dicks" are MBD's (multiple bad dicks) and show traits from several of the "Bad Dick" categories. MBD's are the *worst* "Bad Dicks" of all. You need to know, I don't think there are any *bad* men, per se. But there are some men who are *bad* for relationships. The nine "Bad Dicks" I describe in my book are as follows:

Floppy Dick – Commitment phobic, ambivalent
Player Dick – Multiple girlfriends, womanizer, Don Juan Casinova
Rigid Dick – Controlling and abusive
Slick Dick – Lying, cheating, manipulative
Selfish Dick – Self centered and narcissistic
Cheap Dick – Moochers and misers
Addicted Dick – Drugs, alcohol, porn, sex and more
Wimpy Dick – Low achievers, lazy, drifters
Closed Dick – Emotionally unavailable, uncommunicative

Throughout this book I will advise you when I feel it is best you get some professional help. When I use the word "counseling" it can mean any type of professional assistance – a counselor, a coach, a minister, a spiritual healer, etc. If you cannot afford to pay for a professional, at least consider getting into a support group of some kind. The most helpful mode of healing for me has been my CODA groups. CODA stands for Co-dependents Anonymous. Most cities have groups every day of the week, and they are completely free.

Hopefully this book will give you some comfort and understanding. Hopefully it will help ease your pain. My goal is to provide you with the best information available to assist you in 1) deciding if you should end it, 2) knowing whether or not you could get back together down the road, 3) knowing how to end it in the most positive, loving way possible, 4) knowing how to accept and let go, 5) getting through the stages of the grieving process in the smoothest, quickest, and most painless way possible, 6) taking care of yourself, and 7) learning your lessons, moving on and thriving.

The greatest act of courage is to be and to own all of who you are— without apology, without excuses, without masks to cover the truth of who you are.

--Debbie Ford

Chapter One: Normal Stages of a Relationship

But let there be spaces in your togetherness and let the winds of the heavens dance between you. Love one another but make not a bond of love; rather let it be a moving sea between the shores of your souls.

---Khalil Gibran

Whether you've been with your mate for three months or thirty years, it's always a loss when the relationship ends. It's a loss of what you had, what you hoped to have, and what you wanted but didn't get. Even if you are the one ending it because you aren't in love with this person any more, there is still a loss. Your main loss is the high hopes you had at one time. "High hopes" can be another way of saying "fantasies." Relationships start out with a high level of fantasy and idealization. Most people put their best foot forward in the beginning. Even though we know there is a "honeymoon period," we still can't help wanting to keep those romantic feelings and experiences alive throughout our lifetime. Unfortunately, we can't keep up our best pretenses forever, and our true selves begin to emerge. Sometimes we don't like the person we see after the honeymoon phase is over.

During this "honeymoon" or "idealization" phase (typically three months to three years) the mental and emotional hooks are buried deep into your brain and you slowly become more and more attached, in love, and in some cases, dependent and/or addicted. You create a dream image of your mate based on his behavior at the beginning of the relationship. You may actually not be in love with this *person*, but rather in love with an *idealized image of this person*, or *the way he was in the beginning*. You may be in love with an imagined fantasy life with this person. It's difficult sometimes to know what you really are attached to.

The first step in determining whether or not you should break up is to separate fantasy and emotion from reality. If you've already determined that you should break up, or have already broken up, you will need to separate fantasy and emotion from reality in order to heal.

Normal Stages of a Love (Dating) Relationship

There are a series of stages most love relationships go through. The following seven stages are the usual progression, with the average amount of time into the relationship that they normally occur. These are "healthy averages," and not every relationship goes through all of these stages, nor in this order, nor for the amount of time I've outlined. For example, some couples say they never went through the conflict stage until after they were married. Some couples go directly from "honeymoon" to "marriage." Some couples go in and out of these stages for many years before they decide to either get married, live together, or break up. Even after couples are married or living together, they will often still go in and out of these stages forever.

Honeymoon: One day to three or four months
Disillusionment: Three months to nine months
The Switch: Three months to nine months
Conflict and Negotiation: Nine months to one year
Plateau: One year to two years
Commitment (engagement and/or moving in together): Two years to two and a half years
Marriage: Two and a half years to three years

I want women to know that it isn't always easy, she explained of the ups and downs of love. But it is all part of our path. We have to trust now that one day it will all make sense.

--Bethenny Frankel

Honeymoon

When you first start dating someone new, someone you really like, it's such a wonderful feeling! Something about pheromones – that indescribable thing that causes your body to create the hormone oxytocin, which thereby creates that euphoric feeling or "high." No one really knows what causes us to have chemistry with a certain person — it has to do with our biological makeup, our past experiences and our particular need/desire at the time. Some think it is completely subconscious and cannot be controlled. However, I do think one can control this, or at least change it over time, with enough insight and cognition. If one notices they have high chemistry with the wrong type of people for example, one can change that. It does take a lot of work though!

During the first few months, this exhilaration is usually very high for at least one partner. If it's shared, it can be amplified many times over, and can be so intense that it causes one to be in a drug-induced state. Oxytocin is a drug, of course, albeit a self-made drug. It can be more addicting than heroin.

This can be the best of times, yet it can also be the beginning of the end of the relationship. This "high" can completely overrule your good judgement and make you do things you would never ordinarily do. Some of the ways it can cause the demise of your "eventual, possible, long term relationship" are:

Sleeping with him too soon (before securing a monogamy agreement)
Calling him, emailing him, texting him
Asking to see him
Inviting him to your home or other place
Showing up at his work or home unannounced
Telling him you really like him, want him, love him, etc.
Become like the female character in the movie **How to Lose a Guy in 10 Days**

Disillusionment

The honeymoon period is over. You begin to see him for who he really is. You start noticing things about him you don't really like. You don't want to say anything because you don't want to spoil the honeymoon. So you start talking to your close friends about some of the things that bother you. By the way, talking to trusted friends is a great way of working through relationship issues. Honestly, your friends and family will give you better advice than any relationship expert could! The only reason people go to relationship or counseling professionals is because they refused to take the good advice of their family and friends. So listen to what they say – it will save you a lot of money down the road!

It's no fun to see the honeymoon end. If only you could stay in denial forever! But you are too smart and savvy for that. You know you need to determine early on if this guy has long term relationship potential. You know you can't waste a lot of time on someone who will never be able to be what you want and need. Pay attention to the things that bother you – from the little annoying things to the BIG RED FLAG things. Maybe you can get past some of the little annoying things, but you cannot get past the BIG RED FLAG things.

You are disillusioned and disenchanted. I remember these feelings all too well. It just *sucks*. To have such high hopes for a relationship – then BAM! He's smashed all your hopes to smithereens. Well, maybe they can be repaired – maybe not. But the first step is to accept that no one is perfect, and everyone has flaws. Most of the time when you leave one guy and find another, <u>you're just exchanging one set of problems for another set of problems</u>. So it's important now to determine if this relationship can be salvaged. I will give you lots more information on how to do that.

Most people who broke up after a long term relationship (one or more years) will tell you they saw the signs during the "disillusionment" phase, but refused to confront them. They "knew" this wasn't going to work – deep down in their gut – but they forged ahead because they wanted the relationship to work so badly. Trust your instincts – they will always serve you well.

Raising relationships is a lot like raising children. I've heard experts say that if you don't discipline your child well by the age of two, you are going to have a very difficult time with this child the rest of your life. It's the same way with relationships. You have to start disciplining him right from the start! Even – yes even in the honeymoon phase! If you tolerate poor behavior once, you're likely to get it again and again. So please, if you haven't already, please start confronting problems head on RIGHT NOW.

I will give you one of my situations as an example. I was in a relationship with a man for ten years. When we first started dating, everything was wonderful, glorious, and fabulous. The earth moved, the sun shone brighter, the moon was full just for us, and I was happier and more energetic than I had ever been. After a few months I began to notice some things. I noticed he stopped calling me every day, and sometimes waited till the last minute to ask me out. Thanksgiving, Christmas and New Years Eve were right around the corner and he hadn't mentioned them. He seemed aloof and inattentive much of the time.

Did I mention any of this to him? Definitely not! I was trying to be a "Good Jane" who never shows her cards or her claws. However, what I didn't realize is that a "Good Jane" is empowered and confident in who she is and what she wants. She speaks up and says what she wants. I just didn't know how to do this then. So time went on without me mentioning anything I didn't like, and accepting the relationship on his terms. I slept with him before securing a monogamous relationship. He never mentioned it, and neither did I. I just "assumed" we were committed and exclusive. Well, we all know the word "assumed" stands for making an "ass of u and me."

He wasn't a player, but was definitely a commitment phobic. I finally got fed up with his undependability and instability and mentioned it to him. Otherwise a very intelligent, verbally gifted man, he just sat there looking dumbfounded. Every time I asked him what he wanted he said, "I don't know." Every time I told him what I wanted he said, "I don't know if I can." These are not the answers we want to hear. I broke up with him based on his inability (or lack of desire) to commit. Of course, then he wanted me more than ever, so we went back and forth for the next nine years. He never committed, not even to giving me one night a week that I could depend on seeing him. TEN YEARS of wasted time! And those were my best child-bearing years!

Now I know that when a woman asks a man what he wants in a relationship, and the man responds with "I don't know," it really means, "I know I don't want what we have." Once I got the "I don't knows" I should have left him where I found him. It didn't matter what the reasons were. He didn't want to commit to me, and that was enough to end it STAT.

People don't change.
They only become more so.

--John Bright-Holmes

The Switch

Not every relationship goes through the "switch" phase, but it is so common that it must be mentioned. The "switch" is when the mate who initially was the "pursuer" now becomes the "distancer," and the mate who initially was the "distancer" becomes the "pursuer." Most dating relationships initially start out with one person more interested than the other. In the best case scenario, this would be the man. The reason this is best is that men tend to be the more resistant entity to get into a serious relationship, and if he has to work hard for you in the beginning, he is more likely to become invested.

      The "switch" is most likely to happen in relationships that started with a BANG. If the relationship started out quick and strong, fierce and passionate, it's likely to end the same way – suddenly – without warning – you'll feel like you've been involved in a "hit and run." It can be devastating, because your emotions are going to extremes so quickly that you can't get a real sense about what happened.

      The "switch" is also common when a man comes on very strong in the beginning, and you resisted his pursuits. I can't tell you how many times I've started dating someone who I wasn't that interested in, yet after he pursued me relentlessly, I started liking him more, thinking maybe I should give him a chance. Then, as soon as I showed that I was interested, he started backing off! This is often the case with players, commitment-phobics, and narcissists. It's an interesting phenomenon. It is well known that people tend to want most what they can't have, and once they have it, they don't really want it. It can be very disturbing and confusing.

      On the other hand, I've certainly been in relationships where I was the more interested party in the beginning, and I pursued men – never a good idea! I would offer him my jewels on a silver platter, without any concern about the consequences to me. I was the "dead dear on the doorstep." If you want to know more about this scenario, read my book ***How to Cure a Commitment Phobic***. Needless to say, it never worked out when I was the initial pursuer. But the interesting thing is that as soon as I stopped showing interest in him, he would turn around and start pursuing me. This was flattering, of course, and if I took his bait and accepted his pursuits, he would again become the distancer. Many couples go round and round, back and forth, on and off, playing the "switcharoo" game throughout their relationship, and this was a ride I didn't want to be on.

The only way to survive the switch is to confront it with your partner, and see if you can work together to resolve it. Each person has a different comfort level with intimacy. Find out what your partner's comfort level is, and determine if you can accept it. If your partner is "hot and cold," as in sometimes wanting a lot of intimacy and other times wanting a lot of distance, this can become "crazy-making." This may be an issue you can work through together in couples counseling.

Real love moves freely in both directions.
Don't waste your time on anything else.

--Cheryl Strayed

Conflict Resolution and Negotiation

Most breakups occur during the "conflict" and "negotiation" stages. Differences and conflicts are inevitable – it's how you deal with them that matters. Some differences can be overcome and negotiated, others cannot. I've heard people say, "I'm just not good at relationships." I think what they really mean is, "I'm just not good at conflict resolution." Most of us didn't learn how to communicate, solve problems maturely, resolve conflict, and negotiate differences in our childhoods. I think this should be a required part of our formal education. Unfortunately, most of us have to learn it from our parents, our environment, our culture, our peers, and our experiences. We use a lot of trial and error. We can really make a mess of things until we learn! And even when we do learn, sometimes our emotions can override what we "know" we should do. And sometimes, try as we might, our partners won't work with us.

Most couples try to solve conflicts in the best way they know how. It usually starts with one of the mates getting hurt or angry about something the other did or did not do. If it's the man, he probably went straight from "hurt" to "angry," as most men do. He probably didn't handle his "angry" too well, as most men don't. The woman responds with too much emotion, which most women do. It usually ends in a "fight," with both mates yelling and/or crying. I'm here to tell you that "fights" are unnecessary and ineffectual. You should never have to yell at each other (unless one of you is in danger of getting hit by an oncoming train!). Screaming, yelling, cursing, and verbally abusing are immature behaviors. They don't belong in love relationships.

<u>Conflict resolution is the most important skill to have if you want a lasting relationship.</u> If you and your partner have not been able to work through differences and conflict, I would strongly suggest seeing a counselor of some type to assist you. If you've tried that to no avail, it just may be that the two of you are too different. If you feel you've tried everything and your partner is unwilling to negotiate or work through problems to resolution, then you should cut your losses now and get out.

Negotiation is about creating win-win compromises. I find that men are not very good at handling criticism and put-downs, but they are good at solving problems. So when you confront your man about something you'd like to change, make sure you don't make him "wrong." There are <u>three entities in a relationship</u>: you, me, and the relationship. Try to introduce the problem as a "relationship problem." For example, you can say something like, "We have a problem. I like to know if we have plans for the weekend a few days in advance so I can prepare, and you like to be more spontaneous. Is there a way we can solve this problem together for the sake of our relationship?" This way he doesn't feel it as criticism and doesn't have to get defensive. You put the "relationship problem" in his lap to solve. Most likely, he will try to come up with some solutions. If he turns it back on you and makes you wrong about it, tell him about the "three entities." If he still doesn't respond well, this is a sign he is self-centered.

Some men will resist and see anything you bring up as "your problem." If he continues to put the problem onto you and refuses to take any responsibility for it, or take any action toward remedying it, he's definitely not workable.

The course of true love never did run smooth.

--William Shakespeare

Plateau

Assuming you've made it through the conflict and negotiation stage, you will eventually get to a "plateau" in your relationship. This will be a period from six to twelve months where you will be getting along pretty well. If you find you never have a "plateau" phase, it means your relationship is much too "rocky." If you cannot get out of conflict and negotiation after six months, you should consider ending this relationship. It either means one or both of you are too immature to resolve your conflicts or your relationship is too conflicted due to too many personality differences.

You've heard the saying, "opposites attract." Well I say, "Opposites attract – and then they attack." It's okay if you have some differences – everyone does. But you don't want someone who is very different from you in many important ways. Studies show that marriages last longer when couples are <u>compatible</u> in most ways. Most importantly, your personalities should be compatible, meaning you like each other and like being with each other. You should <u>enjoy</u> being with your partner more than anyone else in the world (except maybe yourself!). The most important "other" things you should be compatible on are:

Whether or not to be exclusive
Whether or not to get married one day
Whether or not to have children one day
Where to live
How you feel about each other's drug/alcohol use
How you spend money and save or invest money
Whether or not you will practice a religion together as a family
What religion you will practice, if you decide to practice
How much time, energy and resources you will put into each other's families
How you will divide money, family activities, life management and jobs
What kind of activities you enjoy doing together or apart
How much time you want to be together or apart

Now, this being said, I want you to know that the number one reason for divorce is not <u>any</u> of these things. The number one reason for divorce is <u>faulty communication and inability to solve problems together</u>. So let's get back to the "conflict and negotiation" stage. Can you solve conflicts and get to resolutions together without too much distress? Can you negotiate compromises regarding your differences? Before you decide whether or not to continue with your relationship, go through the above list together. See if you can get to an agreement on these things. If not, your relationship is doomed.

Truth is everybody is going to hurt you.
You just gotta find the ones worth suffering for.

---Bob Marley

Commitment

Now is the time to think about getting engaged and/or moving in together. Personally, I think it is a good idea to live together for a year before you get married, because you don't really know a person until you live with them. Getting married is probably the most important decision you'll ever make in your lifetime. I say this because being with a good mate you like, love and enjoy will bring you the most satisfaction that life can give (other than your relationship with yourself and God). Being with a mate who causes you distress much of the time will give you the most unsatisfying life possible. You really need to look at your lifestyles and personalities and whether or not you think you will be compatible over the long haul. Living together gives you an advantage in that it helps you see things more objectively. This is a huge decision – one you cannot rely on your heart or emotions to make.

Yes, you could say to me, "Oh, Dr. Lyn, I don't need to know him that long," or "I don't need to live with him first. If things don't work out we can always get a divorce." Well, yes, you can always get a divorce. But I'm here to help you prevent a divorce. Why should I care? Because I know from experience that <u>going through a divorce is one of the most painful things a person can ever go through</u> – not just emotionally, but also physically and financially. Especially if you have children. It was the most painful, difficult thing I have ever been through and I wouldn't wish that upon anyone!

Ask ten people who have been divorced if they would think or do things differently next time around. Ask those ten people to tell you about how difficult divorce was for them and their children. Ask them how much stress and distress it caused. I'm betting you'll take this decision a little more seriously after that!

Within a year of dating, the topic of life-long commitment should come up. It's best if the man brings it up – after all, a woman wants a man who wants her and only her. If he never brings it up within a year, he probably doesn't want it, or has serious doubts about it. If you have a specific timeline for when you want to secure that commitment, as in living together, getting engaged, getting married, or having children, you should <u>tell him about it now</u>. I think a year is a good amount of time for someone to know if he/she wants to be with this other person long term. I think two years is the longest I would wait. Except for some circumstances such as wanting to finish college, wanting to be more financially secure, or living far apart (i.e., job takes one of you away, military, etc.) couples usually start planning their life-long commitment within the first two years of their relationship.

Most couples who get engaged have about a six month to one year engagement before they "tie the knot." This should give you more time to work out differences, problems, solutions and compromises. It also gives you each time to work through any commitment anxieties that may arise. I think pre-marital counseling is a great idea. Again, this being the most important decision in your life, it deserves a little help from experts, don't you think?

Getting married and planning a wedding is actually one of the most stressful times in life. <u>Change is always stressful – even if you perceive it as positive</u>. Believe me, this is a HUGE change for you! Even if you're already living together and will remain in the same home, in the same jobs, and the same lifestyle, there will be changes. The biggest change is that of "perception." Even though I lived with my husband for a year before we married, once we got married he started treating me differently. He subconsciously felt he now "had" me so he didn't have to work for me anymore. He stopped being romantic, stopped asking me out on dates, stopped giving me gifts, stopped doing things for me, stopped calling or texting me just to check in, started working more, and basically stopped paying attention to me. I was devastated! How could I have possibly known this would happen – this enormous change in behavior – once we married?

I must take some responsibility here. Once I really noticed this change, confronted it, and got into marriage counseling, I realized that this was never an issue that had come up in our seven year relationship. In fact, there were a lot of other issues that hadn't come up, and that we had pushed under the rug. We hadn't gone to pre-marital counseling because I was in denial. I wanted the picture-perfect ("Kodak") relationship so badly that I refused to even acknowledge any underlying problems. Hence the very painful divorce five years later (with child). Please don't make the same mistake I did.

Speaking of marriage counseling, I am all for it! Even if you have a good marriage, there are bound to be issues that come up that, if not confronted now, will continue to rear their ugly heads. If you want to keep a great relationship, it's best to have a good counselor on retainer, just as you would an attorney or an accountant. You've invested a whole lot of time, energy and resources into this relationship. You need to maintain it, just as you would any other valuable investment.

Here's the one and only way to stay in relationship. *Commitment.* You must commit to the relationship. You must commit to staying together, no matter what (except certain non-negotiable things which I'll explain later). There are three parts of a relationship – you, me and *the relationship*. It is *the relationship* that you are committing to, each and every day.

Three things cannot be hidden:
The sun, the moon and the truth.

--Buddha

Chapter Two: When the Dream Dies

A dream is a wish your heart makes.

--Cinderella

Fairy Tales

Whether you've been dating a few months to a few decades, when a relationship ends, dreams die. It is a death of what one had wished and dreamed for. Letting go of the dream is very painful. But dreams are not reality and wishes don't make things come true. The only way to handle the pain of broken dreams is to put yourself back into a state of reality.

We were raised on fairy tales and "happily ever afters." Many people, especially women, read lots of romance novels, watch romance movies, and follow romances on TV soap operas and reality TV shows. The more of these types of things you've immersed yourself in, the harder it's going to be for you when your fairy tale doesn't end happily.

Most of the time, one or both partners begins the relationship operating on the "Dream Image." When one partner starts to change gradually, becoming colder or more uncaring, or one gradually see flaws and faults, one may remain blinded by their strong feelings towards the dream image. <u>One or both partners may have been in love with something that was never reality</u>. One partner may have created a dream image of their partner based on their behavior at the beginning of the relationship. As time goes by, they slowly start to realize their view of their partner is a false one. This process can take long time.

What you wish more than anything is that your partner would love you as much and in the same ways you love him or her. This is very natural. If we love someone we wish that person would love us back, otherwise we are unhappy. There are many definitions of love, however. Many of the men I have been with say they loved me, and I believe they loved me as much as they could love anyone, yet it wasn't in a way that could cause me to *feel loved*. This is extremely important. The man you want to spend your life with needs to be one who can consistently cause you to *feel loved*.

Expectations

Expectations are premeditated resentments.

--Anonymous recovery quote

Perhaps your dreams, images, and wishes were simply too high of *expectations*. If you did spend a lot of time absorbed in romance novels and movies, you may have far too high of expectations. These movies, books and TV shows are geared toward women's interests, as that is who consumes them. Women tend to love romance. Men generally are not very good at romance. They may say they like it, but don't demonstrate it. Most men are pretty lazy when it comes to romance and relationships.

However, most men will tell you, they do want to please you, and you just need to show them how. Make sure you've communicated clearly what you want and need from your partner before you decide he isn't going to come up to the plate. You may need to be very specific. I never wanted to have to tell a man how to please me, because then if he did those things, I would simply think he was only doing them because I told him to and not because he really wanted to. We all want our men to do things for us because they have an internal drive to do them. What I've found is that most men do have an internal drive to do things for us, but what they think of isn't what we're thinking of. They may think a new garbage disposal is exactly what we need to feel loved, and we are only thinking about him bringing us flowers. So you have to make sure you've told him what you want before you bail on him.

I had been dating John a few months and Valentine's Day was coming up. I didn't say anything about it because of course, I wanted to see what he would do. He never mentioned it. He called me on V-Day saying he was going to hang out with his "buddy" that night. I was furious. I asked him if he was aware it was V-Day. He said he wasn't. I asked him if he'd like to make it up to me. He said he would, and offered to make dinner for me the next night at my home. He showed up with food but no gift – no flowers, no candy, no wine, no jewelry – nothing. Nothing special – it was just like any other date. I was disappointed to say the least.

It was very difficult for me, but I knew I had to muster up the strength to tell him I was hoping for more. I didn't want to seem like a spoiled brat with overly high expectations, but I didn't want to suffer in silence either. So I asked him in my nicest way, "John, have you been with other women on V-day?" He replied, "Yes." I asked, "Did they ever tell you they wanted their man to figure out a way to romance them and make them feel special on this day?" He said, "No." So I went on to explain how I would like to be romanced, and that I don't think I'm all that different from most women, except that I will say it and they will hold it in and get resentful." He said he appreciated my honesty and would try to do better.

Well, John never did do better, so I had to let him go. For me, romance is a non-negotiable. It doesn't have to be exactly like the books or movies, but he has to give it a good effort. If he's lazy when it comes to holidays, birthdays, and special occasions, he's going to be lazy in the relationship – period.

So here's my point. You can't have hidden dreams, fantasies and expectations. You must tell your partner how you want to be treated. Of course you need some room for compromise, and you need some patience. Men usually take longer to process your words and take action. But within a few weeks, if he/she does come up to the plate, he/she is not for you.

I was thinking' 'bout her, thinking' 'bout me
Thinkin' 'bout us, what we gon' be
Open my eyes, it was only just a dream.

--Lines from the song *Just a Dream* by Nelly

Chapter Three: How to Know If You Should Break Up

*If you do what you've always done,
you'll get what you've always got.*

--Mark Twain

Generally, when you first start to wonder if you should leave him, you should. A self-respecting woman would not put up with a bad relationship. If he is showing bad behaviors, he is showing BAD CHARACTER and BAD MORALS. I normally am not quick to judge, as I seek first to understand, but in the case of selfishness, abusiveness, addiction, lying and cheating, I don't have much empathy or patience. I see these character traits as RWMD's and I don't believe you have a prayer for a good, long-term relationship. If your man has bad character, I beg of you, "Run, Bambi, Run!"

1. The longer you stay with a man with poor moral character, the harder it will be on you to break it off. Your emotions are too important to allow yourself to go down any further. You need to protect yourself. The best way to protect yourself is to live by your standards. Self-respect is more important than having a man in your life just for the sake of having a man in your life.

People show you who they are by their actions. Many women "overlook" bad behaviors because they hold on to a fantasy. They believe in the "Kodak image" of the perfect relationship – the relationship the WANT to have rather than the relationship they really have. You have to get out of denial and see things for what they are, not what you want them to be. Being lied to or cheated on is betrayal. Betrayal is one of the most painful things anyone can ever go through. Unfortunately, betrayal is quite common in our society. The good news is, countless people have survived betrayal, and you can too. If you have been betrayed, please get some professional help so you can heal and move on with dignity and an open heart.

If you are married with children, this will be the most difficult decision you have ever faced. You owe it to your children to try everything you can before ending it. If you are married without children, it will be a little easier, but still very difficult. There is a huge expectation in our society that marriage is forever.

Even though 50% or more marriages end in divorce, there is always that feeling that you SHOULD stay married, no matter what. You SHOULD keep your wedding vows – "Til Dealth Do Us Part." You have to get the "shoulds" out of the way before you can make a rational decision that is best for you in the long run.

How do you know if you should get a divorce? I will cover this more later, but for now I will say that only you can know whether divorce is your best option. You have the answers to all your questions deep down inside of you.

People play the 'what if?' game. Play the game but answer the question, 'what if?' The answer is, 'I'll be fine. I've gotten through it before. I'll get through it again because I believe in me. I'm betting on me.'

--Dr. Phil

Your Five Guiding Forces

When it comes to relationship commitment, we should think about it seriously and try to base our decision on rational thought. We have five guiding forces inside of us that assist us in making relationship decisions: our "head" (brains, logic, and intelligence), our "gut" (intuition), our "heart" (emotion, desire, passion), our "chi" (life force, power, strength) and our "genitals" (chemistry, sexual arousal). In regards to relationships, most people make mistakes when they lead with their "heart" or "genitals" and follow with their "gut" and their "head" and never even use their "chi."

The best way to make relationship choices is to lead with your "head," then use your "gut," then your "chi," then your "heart," and last, your "genitals." Write this down and read it over and over, every day. Your "head" is your brain and your intellect. Your "gut" is your instincts and inner knowing. Your "chi" is your life force. Your "heart" is your emotions. Your "genitals" is your physical attraction. If men would use this method in the order I've described, they would make better choices as well.

Always lead with your "head." Sometimes your brain knows exactly what to do, and sometimes it is confused. If you're in a state of confusion, you need more information. Ask more questions. Ask the five people in your life who know you the best. Get as much information as you can so you can make an intelligent (not impulsive) decision.

Next, you need to trust your instincts (your "gut"). Your instincts are a feeling you get that something is right or not, good or bad. It is not an emotional feeling, it is more of a sense. Some call it the sixth sense. Some call it our "soul" or the "God within." Everyone has it (or can cultivate it) but not everyone listens to it. I have found that prayer and meditation help me to get in touch with that deeper part of me that KNOWS. Inside each of us is a "knowing." It is way down deep in our core. Get in touch with your soul by taking time to think, meditate, or just relax.

As the saying goes, "All is fair in love and war." Love is sometimes like war. The Greeks created Goddesses of War because they realized that women were the fiercer sex. Women do hold all the power, but unfortunately, they don't realize it, and give their power over to men. To win this war, <u>you must be a lover and a fighter</u>. You must use all your strength, energy and endurance (your "chi"). You must claim your prize as rightfully yours. If this man is not your prize, you need to look elsewhere. You cannot be lazy – you must work it until you either get what you want, or decide it's futile and pull out.

The Nine Worst and Nine Best Character Traits for Relationships

In my book, *Bad Dick, Good Jane: How Good Girls Get Bad Boys to Behave, Fall in Love and Commit*, I explain the nine worst kinds of men (Bad Dicks) to be in a relationship with. These are:

Floppy Dick: Commitment phobic, undependable, ambivalent
Player Dick: Womanizers, multiple partners
Stiff Dick: Rigid, controlling, abusive
Slick Dick: Lying, cheating, manipulating, con-artist
Selfish Dick: Self centered, narcissistic
Addicted Dick: Drugs, alcohol, sex, porn and more
Limp Dick: Low achieving, lazy, wimpy, drifter
Cheap Dick: Moochers and misers
Closed Dick: Emotionally unavailable, uncommunicative

If you're not sure if your partner falls into any of these categories, read my book. In each chapter I give you a continuum from mild to severe. If he's manageable, I tell you how to do it. If you've tried all my strategies and he's still not manageable, you need to walk.

The nine best character traits for relationships are:

Honesty
Trust
Integrity
Dependability
Responsibility
Cares about your feelings
Desires to please you
Emotionally mature and open
Ability to solve problems calmly and objectively

The 3 "A's"

Here's an easy test I use to determine if a guy is "in" or "out." The three "A's" are:

Abuse
Adultery
Addiction

Abuse stands for any type of abuse – emotional, verbal or physical. If your partner has become verbally or emotionally abusive, you need to put a stop to it immediately and let him know you will NEVER tolerate it. If he does it again, you either need to get into couples counseling or leave. Physical abuse is not to be tolerated EVER. Use the saying, "Burn me once, shame on you, burn me twice, shame on me." Don't let him burn you twice. Once is enough to know that this is just the beginning of much more and much worse. Don't give him another chance. Get out and protect yourself as soon as you possibly can.

Adultery stands for cheating, lying and stealing. These are character traits that are deeply rooted in one's personality, and cannot be changed unless the person *wants* to change and gets into treatment. If your man has cheated on you, I say, it's OVER. If you really want to try to salvage the relationship you'll need to get professional help. But if he attends as a reluctant partner, beware. He is not going to change. He needs to be the one with tons of remorse who calls and makes the appointment. Personally, I would only see him in the counselor's office for the first year of treatment. Research shows it takes at least a year to change this type of behavior, if ever.

Addiction stands for any type of addiction that causes potential harm to others, i.e., drugs, alcohol, sex, porn, gambling, shopping, sports, work, etc. We live in an addictive society, so it's difficult to find someone with no addiction whatsoever. It becomes a problem when the addiction causes the person to lie, cheat or steal. It becomes a problem when the addiction is more important than your relationship. It becomes a problem when it results in dishonesty or low integrity. It becomes a problem when you feel he loves his addiction more than you. Again, even for someone who is highly motivated, it takes at least a year in recovery for that person to have a chance at lasting change.

Most other issues should be able to be worked on and worked through in a normal, healthy relationship. If you still aren't sure, please see a relationship counselor or coach and get some advice. At least ask the five closest people in your life to give you their honest opinion. Often the people who love us and care about us can see things that are hurting us more than we can see it. If all your friends and family are telling you he's not right for you – trust me—*he isn't.*

If you believe that feeling bad or worrying long enough will change a past or future event, then you are residing on another planet with a different reality system.

--William James

What If I'm Ambivalent About Breaking Up?

Most people are ambivalent for a while before they make a decision. That's okay. It helps you to see your situation more clearly if you understand why you feel the way you do towards your partner. If you are feeling depressed and sad due to problems in your relationship, it is often difficult to judge the situation clearly. You may feel you are in love him, and if you end the relationship your life will be empty and lonely. You may feel that even though your relationship with him is not perfect you still want to hold on to it, since you believe you might never find another person who you can love as strongly as you think you love him.

Many women get to the point where they give their men ultimatums such as, "show me you love me like you did in the beginning or I'll leave." Ultimatums make men angry. If they do give in to an ultimatum, it may be very short-lived, or they may become very resentful and either aggressively or passively aggressively get revenge.

What you should do instead is to <u>tell a man who you are, what you want, and what you are going to do</u>. Simple, right? Men respond well to women who do this, just as children respond better to parents who do this. <u>Men want standards and want to know your standards</u>. You need to speak in simple truths. For example, "I am not the kind of woman who waits years to see if a man will commit. I want a committed relationship that leads to marriage. I give this relationships one year at most and if you don't know you want me by then, I will need to move on."

Remember that we cannot expect men to make us happy and complete. We cannot expect them to meet all our emotional needs. He can contribute to your happiness and sense of peace, but happiness is a process that you create for yourself. We need to think more in terms of "feeling good" rather than "being happy." It's important that we feel good about ourselves most of the time. If this man doesn't cause you to feel good about yourself, you need either get some counseling or find a man who does. You deserve to be happy.

If you think there may be hope for your relationship or you don't have the emotional strength to end it, yet you have not been able to resolve certain problems together, you should at least insist on couples counseling. Personally, I believe your best vantage point is to "<u>talk and walk</u>." I think it's best to tell him that your relationship has some serious problems and you would like to go to couples counseling with him. If he refuses you will respect that decision. However, you also have choices, and you choose to be healthy and since <u>your relationship can only be as healthy as the least healthy member</u>, his decision to remain unhealthy forces you to make a difficult decision. You have decided that you want to be healthy and want to be in a healthy relationship. Therefore, if he doesn't choose to get healthy (by accepting professional help), you will need to leave. You will not see him or speak to him unless it is at a counselor's office. Period.

He will likely become resistant and defensive and say something like, "Fine, I don't like a lot of things about you either, and you have a problem with (whatever) so who are you to tell me I need help? If you don't like me for who I am, go ahead and leave, I don't care." All you need to say in response is, "Thank you for sharing your feelings with me. I would love to work on all of these things with you. Please call me when we can meet together with a professional." Then you WALK. You don't argue, plead, beg, cry, scream, or call him later apologizing. You stay away until he surrenders and asks you to meet him at the counseling office. Or not.

Yes, you are taking a risk of losing him and losing the relationship right here. This will be a difficult thing to do, especially if you know losing him will put you into a place of pain and grief. Yet deep down in your heart you know it's your only chance to ever have a healthy relationship with him. You have to muster up the courage and strength to do it and follow through with it. If you don't think you can endure the pain or stay away from him, do not go through with the request yet. Get some counseling or coaching to get you stronger before you do it. Just like with parenting, when we continually make idle threats to our children, they learn not to believe anything we say and walk all over us.

If he refuses counseling, you should refuse to see him or talk to him (do what you said you were going to do!). If he keeps calling you, writing you, begging you to give him another chance, simply say, "I will give you another chance when we get into counseling and we can discuss where we want our relationship to go."

Courage is the power to let go of the familiar.

--Raymond Lindquist

Should We Just Take a Break?

You have the right to take a break from a relationship any time you want, for any reason. You do need to tell that person why you want the break, however. It wouldn't be fair to just stop contact without explanation. Many couples take breaks in their relationships and find it is very helpful. My experience has been (and most of those I've consulted) that whatever the reason is that you took the break for the first time, will keep coming back up, no matter how many breaks you take. So you need to know that a "break" will not necessarily change anything. It will just give you some time apart. Maybe that's all you need. If so, be honest about it.

People are creatures of habit, and even when they have the best intentions to change their behaviors, the old habits tend to creep back up as soon as the pressure's off, or the pressure's on. Be careful you don't get on the "yo-yo" cycle (I'll explain later) because it's very difficult to get off. Usually the first time you break up with a man should be the last.

Think about this. People in our lives are either brining us UP or bringing us DOWN. There is very little in between. Use this as your meter. If your partner is not trying to bring up the relationship, i.e., making it better, improving it, making it more interesting or fun or meaningful, then they are not really into it. If you or your partner are not bringing up the relationship the majority of the time, then either one or both of you lacks the passion to make your relationship great. If there is no passion – no fire – no "she's the one and I'm going to make this work come hell or high water," then what's the point? If there is no fire, there is no glue. Relationships are difficult enough in this world and without some kind of fire to keep it alive, it will eventually die out.

Reset your "breakup" maximum to ONE.

--Greg Behrendt, Author of *He's Just Not That In To You*

What If He's a Great Guy but I'm Just Not IN to Him?

This is by far the most common relationship problem I hear from women. She starts dating a really great guy, who either looks good, or looks good on paper, or who is extremely nice, sensitive, and generous, or all of the above. Soon she realizes she's not attracted to him sexually. She doesn't feel any chemistry. She doesn't feel a connection on a deeper level. She might like him as a friend, and have a huge amount of admiration and respect for him, but there's no spark. She's just not that IN to him.

Usually she feels this guy likes her more than she likes him. First of all, it's normal to want what we can't have, and most men love a challenge. So if you act like you're not that in to him, he may just want you MORE. He may try harder and sometimes we see this as a weakness. Most women want the alpha male who is confident, aloof, and a little bit hard to get. The man who wants us <u>that bad</u> must not be <u>that good</u>.

Sometimes she keeps going out with him, hoping she will eventually feel something. Sometimes she just stops seeing him without any explanation. I certainly have been here, many times, and I really feel for anyone in this situation. It's so difficult to find a really good guy, so we feel bad, ashamed, angry and guilty when we do find him and we don't want him. Try as we might, we just can't get into it. As I'll explain later, it is almost impossible to change your sexual chemistry with a person from zero to WOW. It is much easier to change your sexual chemistry with a person from WOW to zero (keep reading!).

Just as I wouldn't be too impulsive to break it off with a guy you are IN to, I wouldn't break it off too quickly with a guy you're not IN to. It's nice to be treated well and have a guy to do things with who you like. It's important though, not to lead him on. Let him know you just want to be friends. I think it's a good idea for a woman who's dating to have a "three-legged stool." This means dating three men at any given time. This keeps you objective and slows down your relationships with all of them. I wouldn't sleep with any of these three men until the one you want the most asks you for exclusivity. Never sleep with a "friend" unless you are sure you don't want a LTCR. The problem with "friends-with-benefits" relationships is that most women will eventually get emotionally involved with any man she sleeps with. If that "friend" lets her down in any way, she may get hurt more than if she hadn't been sleeping with him. Protect your emotions!

Cold Hearted
By Paula Abdul

How come he can tell you you're
Always number one without a doubt
(He's one cold snake)
When he is always squirmin'

*Like a little snake under a rock
(No give, all take)
You've been workin' on the love
And he's been only playing undercover all the while
(One smooth sharp tongue)
Take a take 'nother look into his eyes
(He just talks)
And you will only see a reptile.*

*He's a cold-hearted snake
Look into his eyes
Oh oh oh
He's been tellin' lies
He's a lover boy at play
He don't play by the rules
Oh oh oh
Girl don't play the fool – no.*

*You're the one givin' up the love
Anytime he needs it
But you turn your back and then he's off and runnin' with the crowd
You're the one to sacrifice
Anything to please him
Do you really think he thinks about you when he's out?*

*He's a cold-hearted snake
Look into his eyes
Oh oh oh
He's been tellin' lies
He's a lover boy at play
He don't play by rules
Oh oh oh
Girl don't play the fool – no.*

*It was only late last night
He was out there sneakin'
Then he called you up to check that you were waiting by the phone
All the world's a candy store*

He's been trick or treatin'
When it comes to true love girl with him there's no one home.

He's a cold-hearted snake
Look into his eyes
Oh oh oh
He's been tellin' lies
He's a lover boy at play
He don't play by rules
Oh oh oh
Girl don't play the fool -- no.

You could find somebody better girl
He could only make you cry
You deserve somebody better girl
He's c-cold as ice.

He's a cold-hearted snake
Look into his eyes
Oh oh oh
He's been tellin' lies
He's a lover boy at play
He don't play by rules
Oh oh oh
Girl don't play the fool – no.

Chapter Four:
How to Handle It When You Are the One to End It

My method is to take the utmost trouble to find the right thing to say, and then to say it with the utmost levity.

--George Bernard Shaw

First I'll discuss how to handle it when you're ending it because you just aren't that IN to him anymore. Next, I'll discuss how to handle it when you are still in love with him but know he's not right for you. Both situations are difficult.

How to End It When You're Just Not That IN To Him

You have been dating for a while, and you were IN to him in the beginning, but now you're not IN to him anymore. This has happened to me many times. After the "honeymoon" period wears off I realize I don't really like him anymore. It often surprises me how my feelings can go from <u>strong infatuation to pure annoyance</u> so quickly. It's much more difficult if you've been intimate with him and especially difficult when you know he loves you. How to let him go? If you've spent a lot of time together, I would start by letting him know the things you enjoyed and appreciated. Then, simply say you don't feel you have enough in common or you aren't feeling a spark. You do not owe him any other explanation. You can't expect him to like it, or be happy about it, but he should at least be respectful.

Sometimes men get very angry when you break up with them, especially if they have started to form an attachment to you. One guy I dated for a few months seemed to take it pretty well when I ended it with him in person. I simply said I didn't feel we were a good match. He gave me a hug and we said good-bye. The next day I got a nasty email from him, basically saying he was in shock and that I was a "phony person." I responded as nicely as I could (an attempt to diffuse his anger), "I understand it may have seemed abrupt to you. I'm very sorry for that, however, I know myself very well and once I knew for sure how I felt I wanted to let you know, so as not to prolong the inevitable. There is really no 'good' way, nor 'good' time, to end a relationship. I try my best to be honest and be who I am with people. I'm sorry if I seemed phony to you. I do wish the best for you."

Thankfully, he never bothered me again. I've had some men keep it up, and at times it has been downright scary. I'll discuss more about this later.

How to End It When He's Not Right (or Good) For You

If you've reached the end of your rope with your man, you may need to end your relationship. Most men will not be the one to end the relationship. 90% of divorces are filed by women. This is because they are not comfortable with any type of emotion, and surely there will be some emotions coming up during a breakup. They also are not comfortable with confrontation and may be too fearful of a possible conflict or emotional outburst. Most men who want to end a relationship will "act out" until you are forced to do their dirty work. If your man has been acting badly for a while, it may be his way of telling you he wants out.

If you really love and want this man, you should not end the relationship until you are sure you have tried everything first to salvage it. Even if you think he wants out – try not to take it personally – it may just mean he started "feeling" too much for you and it scared him. Always offer couples counseling first. If he absolutely refuses to go, even after you've set up an appointment for the two of you, then okay, I must admit, there's probably not much hope, at least not right now.

When/if you decide you need to break up with him, you should do it in person rather than through text, phone, or email. This shows him respect and an opportunity to respond to your concerns and desires. The exception to this would be if you are fearful that he may explode into a rage and become abusive in any way. Be prepared that he may walk out the door at the first hint of your breaking up speech. If this should happen, don't take it personally, don't worry about it, and don't try to stop him. Let him walk. You don't have to have your say. You don't have to tell him how you feel. Trust me, he already knows.

Now let's assume he does stick around for the bad news. First, state what you appreciate about him and the relationship. For example, if he helped you through the death of a relative, or took your dog to the vet for you, thank him for his support. If you appreciated how he gave you a nice card or flowers once, or he cooked you dinners, or whatever, let him know. Let him know what first attracted you to him and why you felt he was worthwhile to invest your time in.

Then tell him when you started noticing that you were different in an important area. Give him examples of the times you tried to talk to him about it and make positive changes that would work for both of you. You can tell him that you have different emotional, spiritual, and/or physical intimacy needs and desires. Try not to make him "wrong" about it. Focus on being "different." Let him know you tried as hard as you could, but it simply became more work than fun for you. Relationships should not be that difficult. Let him know you enjoyed a lot of your time together, but you need to move on now.

I can pretty much guarantee that you won't be the first woman who has broken up with him or expressed her frustration to him for the same reasons. And you probably won't be the last. It usually takes three to five women to tell a man the same thing, plus maturity, before they "get it." Some men never do, and that's a shame, because they will end up alone – maybe depressed and alone.

If you tried everything you could and he didn't want to change, you don't have to feel bad or guilty about leaving him. You may feel sad for a while – that's normal. You may want to call him and see him again – that's normal too. But if you ever want to be in a happy, healthy relationship you must break the chain. You must not accept a life of frustration and pain. You must not find another unhealthy man to replace him. You must move forward toward your happiness!

According to Oprah, you don't owe men an explanation. You can simply say that you have come to believe that you are not a good match. You may be willing to tell him what the main differences are, and how you've attempted many times to work them out, but the two of you have been unable to do so. Don't blame him. Don't blame yourself. There are three entities in a relationship – you, me, and "the relationship." Remember, it is the third entity that isn't working – the relationship.

Can We Remain Friends?

A lot of women tell me they want to break up with this man, but they still want to remain "friends." Can you still be friends? Oprah says, "If a relationship ends because he was not treating you as you deserve then heck no, you can't be friends. A friend wouldn't mistreat a friend." I recommend you give it a year with no contact. A lot can change in a year. If you really want to know what might have changed with him ask him to call you in a year. Do not tell him you'll call him, and by no means should you contact him.

This being said, it is important to forgive. You need to forgive yourself as well as your lover. Forgiveness doesn't mean forgetting, it just means that you aren't bound by resentment, anger and hostility. You cannot heal if you are caught up in a continual blame cycle. Holding on to resentment is like holding on to a hot coal – it only burns YOU. You don't need to throw hot coals on your ex. Throw them into the ocean and let them float away.

Everything is just as it needs to be. And if we would forgive, Our minds and hearts would open and we could see another possibility.

--Iyanla Vanzant

Personal Boundaries

Wherever you are in life, whatever you have in life, right now, is due to the choices you've made. You created the life you're living by the people you chose to let in and the people you chose to leave out. You've chosen based on your <u>personal boundaries</u>. Your boundaries are like walls or borders, where you begin and other people leave off. Just as your brain is protected by tissue, blood and bone, you protect yourself through your boundaries.

A boundary is a limit you set to protect you and your integrity. You only have so much time, energy and resources. You have to make choices about how you'll spend your time and whom you'll choose to spend it with. Healthy boundaries are permeable. They allow some things in and don't allow other things in. What you choose in is about your CHOICES. Boundaries keep you in tact and create a manageable life – or not. Boundaries are about your SURVIVAL.

The best defenses are solid emotional fences.

--Oprah Winfrey

When to Amputate

When you break up with a man you've been intimate with for a long time, it can feel like an amputation. Sometimes, the only way to stop the "bleeding" is to "amputate." When doctors are making a decision as to whether or not to amputate a person's limb, they base their decision making on the best interest of the patient's <u>overall health and well-being</u>. This is what you should do also. You need to look at the <u>big picture of your life</u>. Is keeping this man in your life causing you distress, upset, or illness? Is having this man in your life keeping you from being as healthy and successful as you could be? Would keeping this man cause you to be unhealthy in any way? Would the loss of this man cause you to be more or less healthy?

Amputating means cutting him out of your life. Your inner self knows whether or not you should do this. Of course, whenever there is an amputation, it takes time for the injury to heal. The body may go through many painful reactions while it is recovering and re-balancing. The patient may go through a period of emotional distress, depression, and despair. They will go through a grieving process just as though they had lost a significant other. It will take time, good medical care, and plenty of social support for the person to fully recover, accept and integrate into their new life. So yes, for a while, you may be in more pain than ever before. Yet for the <u>long run</u>, you may have just saved your life.

You Don't Know a Man Until You've Broken Up With Him

I know I previously stated, "You don't really know a man until you've lived with him," but now I'm going to up the ante. You don't really know a man until you've broken up with him. I can't tell you how many times I've broken up with a man (or simply said I wasn't interested in dating him anymore) only to see a completely different side of him than I had ever seen before! Most men don't take this conversation well. Most men, no matter how nicely you put it, see it as rejection. Some see it as betrayal. Some refuse to accept it. Sometimes it brings out the WORST in them.

This is the time you need to be very careful and aware of his reaction. You will find out how emotionally mature or immature he is at this point, if you haven't already. An emotionally healthy man will be able to hear you, accept it, thank you for your honesty, and move on. He may feel sad for a while, but he won't take it out on you. He won't try to talk you out of it, get defensive, try to get revenge, or become aggressive or passive aggressive in some way (such as not giving you back your things).

An emotionally unhealthy man will either become defensive, angry, or revengeful. If he isn't able to accept it, he will not be able to let go. He may call you and harass you. He may become obsessed with you. He may stalk you. He may threaten you. He may become aggressive and hostile toward you. This is when you must realize you (and your children if you have them) are in danger and take measures to protect yourself. Most murders in the U.S. happen <u>between lovers</u>. <u>Most murders between lovers happen within a few months after a breakup – especially when one partner has started seeing someone new</u>. I'm not trying to scare you, I'm just trying to help you see the warning signs and protect yourself.

I set fire to the rain,
Watched it pour as I touched your face,
Well, it burned while I cried
'Cause I heard it screaming out your name.

--Lines from the song *Set Fire to the Rain* by Adele

Chapter Five:
How to Handle It When Your Mate Is the One to End It

As I've said, it is rare that the man ends the relationship. Men generally are not comfortable with conflict and "endings," and will usually "act out" until you are forced to end it. However, there are cases where the man will own up to not wanting the relationship any more, and be honest with you about it. If you like this guy, it always hurts, even if you have only been dating a few weeks. The longer you've been together, the more difficult it is.

Hopefully, his news will not come as a shock to you. Ideally, you would have already tried working out your problems, preferably with a professional, and the two of you would come to the conclusion together that it isn't going to work. You would then have the support of a trained professional to assist you through the grieving process. But we don't live in an ideal world, and most likely, you will be a little stunned when it happens. The most important thing is that you keep your <u>dignity</u>.

I have explained how men often react to your breakup news, and it's not usually in a dignified or healthy way. Now, I will explain how <u>women</u> often react to his breakup news, and it's not usually dignified or healthy either! Most women get very emotional – that is, they cry, scream, beg, plead, and verbally attack. Women often become "drama queens" and fly off into a rage. They become emotional wrecks and make ugly scenes. All of these reactions are unhealthy and self-destructive.

Once I dated a guy for nine months and things were proceeding very well. Out of nowhere one day he called to tell me he was going back with his ex-wife because their daughter was suffering due to their divorce. I was completely shocked, since he had downgraded this woman during our whole relationship. I took a deep breath and thanked him for his honesty and told him I thought it was an honorable thing to do for the sake of their daughter, and I wished him the best. I got off the phone as quickly as I could, called my best friend and cried and screamed to her! I ranted and raved and got all my anger and upset out. I'm sure you can imagine how much I would have liked to REAM him for this. I wanted to tell him, "Good luck with that!" I wanted to tell him he'd be sorry, because it would never work out with her and eventually he'd want me back and I'd be gone! But I had the "where-with-all" to somehow collect myself and keep my dignity. It may have felt good at the time to "give it to him" but I knew one day I'd regret it. I knew I may see him again and I'd want things to be civil. Even if I never saw him again, I wanted to keep my own self-respect.

Of course it turned out to be a blessing in disguise (it always is!) because six months later he called to tell me they had broken up and wanted to see me again, and I was able to say sorry, I'm seeing someone else now. Then I heard he had gone back with her, and to this day they are on-again-off-again. I certainly don't need that in my life!

I happen to not believe that there is only one right person for each of us. Don't ever tell yourself you've lost the one person you were destined to be with forever. There's nothing magical about one person. He's just a man. Nothing more – nothing less. In reality, there are plenty of people with whom each of us is potentially compatible. Resist thinking you've lost your one true soul mate.

He Breaks Up With You But Can't Let You Go

Here's a big problem. He's the one that broke it off, yet he can't let go. He keeps calling you to say he misses you. He wants to see you. He needs to see you. He thinks he might have made a mistake. It is very tempting to believe this guy and want to see him again. Seeing him again would relieve your pain and anxiety. Seeing him would put a salve on the wound. Maybe he really does miss you. Maybe he realizes he really did lose the best thing he ever had.

Don't be misled. Of course he misses you. No matter who does the breaking up, each partner feels a loss. Each partner will grieve this loss. If he's grieving, and doesn't know how to grieve in a healthy way, he may think that all he needs is to see you again – hold you – kiss you—make love to you – and everything will be all better. And it may, for a little while. But as soon as he's gotten his "fix" he will leave, and nothing will have changed. You'll be the victim left behind – again.

This is a very common scenario with players and commitment phobics. They can't commit to being with you but they can't commit to being without you. They will suck you into their twisty-turny ambivalence until you've dangled in the wind so long you finally let go. Please have more dignity than this. He's not being fair to you and he's wasting your time. The next chapter should help you prevent this situation, or assist you in stopping the cycle if it's already happening.

Don't be flattered that he misses you. He should miss you. You are deeply missable. However, he's still the same person who just broke up with you. Remember, the only reason he can miss you is because he's choosing, every day, not to be with you.

--Greg Behrendt, *He's Just Not That In To You*

The Addictive Relationship

Addictive relationships typically go through a process that starts with innocent attraction. This phase quickly turns into infatuation. Hungry for love, the relationship addict feels exhilarated and blinded. This turns into an excessive preoccupation with the loved one involving hours of fantasy about how the relationship might turn out. This fantasizing can happen in healthy relationships to a certain extent, but the difference with addictive relationships is when fantasy thoughts control one's mind while rational thought is abandoned.

Love addicts then project all their dreams of happiness onto the loved one. These fantasies trigger the dependency phase of the relationship. The addict then develops fear that the relationship could come to an end, and with it, all hope for a happy life. These fears lead to an obsessive quest to hold on to the lover at any cost – even if it means using control and manipulation.

At this point, the relationship usually begins to deteriorate. The addict puts so much energy into molding the relationship into what he/she needs that the other person begins to feel smothered. The loved one may express resentment in the form of lying, cheating, taking for granted or abusing the love addict. This puts a severe strain on the relationship and causes the addict to try even harder. A vicious cycle begins.

The love addict keeps on trying, at all cost, to keep alive the dream of experiencing happiness through the other person. When the pain becomes too immense they go into denial, acting as if everything is going well. They are not able to see where the true problem likes, which is in their own unmet needs and addictive process. They idealize the relationship, even though it is becoming more emotionally volatile and not meeting the needs of either partner.

The most difficult relationship to end is the addictive relationship. From my experience and research, the best and most effective way to stop any addiction is to go "cold turkey." This means to STOP completely. This means NO CONTACT with him whatsoever, of any kind. Some women will need to get a restraining order in order to do this – but unfortunately I've seen dozens of women go to a LOT of TROUBLE to get a no-contact order and then break it themselves due to the extreme power of their addiction. If this man has threatened to harm you or your children, or has harmed you or your children, you need to get a restraining order immediately! This must be your number one priority! Your safety and the safety of your children is the most important thing in your life. It must become MORE IMPORTANT than your addiction.

Before you make a decision to STOP all contact, you need to be CONVICTED and COMMITTED. You cannot waffle on this at all. As the saying goes, "give him an inch and he'll take a mile." You must be very sure. You will need to enlist the support of allies. Your allies will be a group of friends, family and/or professionals who know you well and have your best interest at heart. The more allies you have, the better. So stock your arsenal, and load up. Alcohol and drug addiction recovery programs have found that social support and sponsors are the most important aspect of recovery. You're going to need your support group more than you will ever know. This group may mean the difference between life and death.

Each member of your support group needs to be committed to your decision as well. You need to ask if they can support you in your decision. Ask for permission to call them when you start to feel weak. Ask what they will do if you "relapse." Relapse is very common, so you need to ask for their support during these times as well. You need to ask them to help you back up if you fall. Ask them to hang in there with you, as it can take one or two years to recover.

Okay, so let's say you've decided to go "cold turkey" and you tell him never to contact you again (or you get a restraining order). You've got your support group in place. 90% of the time he will still try to contact you, and he may be relentless. He knows exactly what to do and say to get you back into contact with him. He will push every vulnerable button you have. You will need to be VERY STRONG about your no contact decision. It may take every ounce of energy you have, but you have to fight this fight by NO CONTACT. By "no contact" I mean NO CONTACT. Do not text him or email him or leave him a voice mail over and over saying please stop contacting me. You are only going to tell him ONCE and MEAN IT. No matter what he does, you cannot give in to temptation – <u>not even once</u>.

You will need to delete him from your life as much as possible, while still maintaining your own life. You will need to avoid the places where he might be. You need to delete his number from your phone. You may need to move away for a while. Sometimes an extended vacation helps. You must be willing to do whatever it takes for you to stay on your no contact program.

Trust me, if you walk away, 90% of the time men come back and ask for another chance. This is because you have all the power now. You hold all the cards. You've got ovaries of steel. You are strong and tough – you look fear in the face and laugh at it. Your only job is to stay strong and keep your word.

If you decide to leave, I think it's best not to start dating for a while. You would benefit from a "dating detox." Patti Stanger, author and host of the popular TV show *The Millionaire Matchmaker*, coined this term. Your "dating detox" would be anywhere from one month to one year, depending on how quickly you recover and adjust. The important thing is that you don't try to replace him with someone new. You need to replace him with YOURSELF. Become your own best friend. This way you'll be able to handle any loss much easier and you won't feel as dependent on a man.

When I have needed to detox from a man in the past what has helped me is to announce to my support group that I am in "Dating Detox." I personally refuse to substitute with other men as I feel I am too vulnerable at this time. I refuse to substitute with drugs or alcohol or food or shopping or any other addictive substance. I substitute with ME. I use this time (usually 3 – 6 months) to focus on myself, self-care, my goals, my career, my friends, my family, my hobbies and activities. I take more baths, I get more facials, I exercise more, I drink more water, smoothies and teas, I get more sleep, I meditate and pray more.

If you want it, take it
I should've said it before
Tried to hide it, fake it
I can't pretend anymore

I only wanna die alive
Never by the hands of a broken heart
Don't wanna hear you lie tonight
Now that I've become who I really am

This is the part when I say I don't want ya
I'm stronger than I've been before
This is the part when I break free
'Cause I can't resist it no more

You were better, deeper
I was under your spell
Like a deadly fever, yeah, babe
On the highway to hell, yeah

Thought on your body
I came alive
It was lethal
It was fatal
In my dreams it felt so right
But I woke up every time

This is the part when I say I don't want ya
I'm stronger than I've been before
This is the part when I break free
'Cause I can't resist it no more
This is the part when I say I don't want ya
I'm stronger than I've been before
This is the part when I break free
'Cause I can't resist it no more

Lines from the song *Break Free*, by Ariana Grande

Chapter Six: The "Yo-Yo' Syndrome

Breaking up is like trying to knock over a vending machine. You have to rock it back and forth a few times until you get that final push.

--Jerry Seinfeld

On Again, Off Again

Don't feel bad – most couples do it. The "yo-yo syndrome" is going back and forth a few times before you finally get the strength to cut it. I'm ashamed to admit how many times I've done it. What I've found is that it never works to go back. Once you've broken up – it's over. There's a great book named *It's Called a Breakup Because It's Broken*. What I've learned from my own "yo-yo" experience is that the reason I broke up with him in the first place, is the same reason I broke up with him again and again.

This is because people are creatures of habit. This is also because people have a certain set of personality characteristics that are pretty well ingrained by the time they are adults. The only way to truly change a personality trait is for the person to WANT to change it, and make a concerted effort to change it. This means getting professional help.

The other main reason people go back and forth is to avoid the inevitable. No one wants to feel the pain of loss. We want to postpone it as long as possible. Getting back together temporarily relieves the anxiety of your impending breakup. It relieves you of the impending pain and grief you must feel after such a loss. It's normal to want to avoid and postpone pain. But eventually, you will need to face it. Because whatever broke you up to begin with will keep rearing its ugly head, and eventually you will KNOW you need to leave. Finally.

Then there's what Jerry Seinfeld calls the "Run-Into -- Fall-Back" syndrome. You just happen to run into your ex somewhere. You think this may be a "sign" that you should see each other again. He looks good, and is very friendly. He asks how you're doing and looks even says he's been thinking about you or has missed you. He says something like, "Can I call you?" or "Can I see you?" Oh how tempting! But you must resist! What usually happens if you see him again is that you "fall back" into a semi-relationship that eventually ends the same way it did last time. It feels great for a little while, then it feels worse than it did before. It's like a bad drug that you have to withdraw from all over again. Just say, "Thanks, but I've moved on."

Most personalities don't change much over time. With a huge amount of effort and support, a person may be able to hold it at bay, as in recovery from an addictive personality. As we know from addictions and recovery research, once an addict – always an addict. The person needs to be in recovery for a very long time, possibly the rest of their lives. So the reason you broke up with him initially will keep rearing its ugly head.

The biggest problem with the "yo-yo" syndrome is that it keeps you stuck in a past that doesn't work for you and prevents you from moving toward a future that does work for you. You cannot be open to receiving a new, good man into your life if you're still holding on to the old one. You cannot be open to new love while you're still hoping to get back the old one. You must let go of the old to make way for the new. You must create "space" for something new and better to come into your life. Trust me, it can only come to you when you have open space for it. Open space means that no other man is in there. He's not in there emotionally, mentally or physically. He's got to GO.

We are never, ever, ever
Getting back together.
Like EVER.

Lines from the song *Never Getting Back Together* by Taylor Swift

Tough Love

The only way to get off the "yo-yo" merry-go-round is to grow some <u>ovaries of steel</u> and get <u>tough love</u> with yourself. You must believe you deserve more than this. You must believe you deserve better than this. You must create space for a better man to come in to your life. You MUST make it a MUST.

*'Cause you keep me coming back for more
And I feel a little better than I did before
And if I never see your face again
I don't mind
'Cause we gone much further than I thought we'd get tonight.*

--Lines from the song *If I Never See Your Face Again* by Maroon 5

Drop the Need for Revenge

If you have felt betrayed by this breakup, it's natural to have some feelings of wanting revenge. You may feel a need to "even the scales." But getting revenge never evens the scales, because anything you do to try to "wound" your ex sill boomerang back to you and make you feel worse. So how can you get out of torment and find yourself again? Forgiveness is the opposite of resentment. Forgive your ex and forgive yourself. Send him love and light and let him go. Now focus on your own self healing.

Here are Depak Chopra's <u>seven worst things you can do and seven best things you can do to move on with your life</u>, as printed in <u>www.Oprah.com</u>, June 6, 2012.

The 7 Worst Things You Can Do

1. Dwelling obsessively on how you were wronged.
2. Turning your pain into an ongoing drama with your ex.
3. Acting erratic and scattered, with no plan for getting better.
4. Mourning your loss obsessively without looking honestly at the hole inside yourself.
5. Talking to the wrong people about your woes, i.e., those who amplify your resentment by egging you on.
6. Idealizing the past – obsessing over the good times that are gone.
7. Letting self-pity and regret dominate your state of mind.

7 Ways to Move On

1. Gain some detachment. Stand back and view yourself as the helper, not the victim.
2. Don't indulge in emotions you cannot afford.
3. Make a plan for emotional recovery and healing.

4. Feel the hole inside and grieve over it – but promise yourself that you will fill it with yourself.
5. Seek a confidant who has survived the same betrayal and has come out on the other side.
6. Work toward a tomorrow that will be better than yesterday.
7. Counter your self-pity by being of service to someone else.

You can heal yourself when you've filled the hole left behind by a betrayal, and you can heal the other person when you sincerely drop the need for revenge.

--Depak Chopra

Chapter Seven: Healthy Grieving

Break the heart and its borders close, accepting no visitors until the worst is over.

--Helen Oyeyemi

Normal Stages of Grieving

The ending of a relationship is a long, slow experience – a set of grieving stages that one goes in and out of, not necessarily in this order:

Denial
Anger
Bargaining
Disappointment, sadness and depression
Acceptance
Healing
Reintegration

Denial

Your period of denial will depend on how much time you had to "prepare" for the breakup. If it comes suddenly, you may have a period of shock, where you don't feel anything. Your mind goes into a state of denial to help protect you from the shock. You may say things like, "I can't believe it! I can't believe this is happening!" The period of shock and denial typically lasts from a few minutes to a few days.

During the denial period you will likely not be able to make much sense of the situation, nor should you make any major decisions about it. Depak Chopra explains that when something happens that we perceive as "bad" or "a problem," we tend to go straight into "constricted consciousness." We tighten up, go within, and may even want to physically curl up into a ball and hibernate for a while. This is normal and can even be healthy. This period allows you to relax so you can get to the next stage of grieving.

Anger

Soon you may find yourself feeling angry. You may be angry at him, at yourself, at others, or at the world. You may find yourself ruminating and asking, "Why?" You are beginning to come out of denial and see the situation a little more clearly (but not clearly, yet). You see the situation from your "pain body" as Eckert Tolle calls it. You see the situation from an egotistical point of view. It's all about ME. Why ME? How could he do this to ME? What did I do to deserve this? Why does this always happen to ME?

Before one can be angry, they must first have been *hurt*. Your anger is coming from a place of hurt. Someone has either wounded you or touched a previous wound that has never healed. The unhealed wound will be the most painful. This may be a "wake-up call" for you to finally get some help for unhealed wounds, so they don't have to keep opening back up. But first, you just need to get in touch with your anger, as you may not be ready yet to feel the pain of the *hurt*.

You may cry, scream, yell, and withdraw during this time. It is healthy to get your feelings out, as long as you aren't taking them out on anyone else, or taking them out on yourself. Depression is anger turned inward. Hostility is anger turned outward. Both of these states are unhealthy if you "act out" physically on them. During this period you may need to go <u>back and forth between inward anger and outward anger</u> until you can see things in a more objective and rational way. It almost always takes "two to tango," so you will need to take some responsibility for the breakup, but you don't need to take it all. Try to see both sides of the story.

Soon you will be able to relax a little more, and you will begin to come out of "constricted consciousness" and move toward "open consciousness."

Bargaining

Not everyone goes through the stage of "bargaining," but it is very common. After a short period of feeling hurt and anger, it's natural to want to be relieved. You subconsciously may try to salve your wound by having some contact with him. You may feel you need to talk to him, see him, or at least write him a letter. You may feel you need to defend yourself. You may feel you want to inflict hurt and pain on him. You may feel you want to get "closure" with him. Whatever your motives are, it's best to wait a while before initiating contact or responding to his contact.

During the "bargaining" stage, women sometimes will try to figure out a way to get him back. It's common to see women change their appearance by losing weight, getting a new hairstyle, working out more, etc. Many women think things like, "If only I were prettier, thinner, more beautiful, more athletic, he will want me more." This is futile, because if he only wants to be with you if you are "prettier," that is a superficial reason which won't last. Many women will say things like, "I'll do anything to have you back in my life!" Of course, we know this is simply desperation talking, and as soon as you are back together, she will revert back to her old behaviors.

Some women become very calculating and manipulative during this time. She may tell him she is sorry, she realizes what she's done wrong, and promises to do better. She may ask him to join her in counseling, go to church with her, or talk to someone else with her. She may do nice things for him. She may do mean things to him. She may become desperate and stalk him. She may do self destructive things to get his attention.

Sometimes her "bargaining" efforts pay off, and she is able to get him to see her again. She may go through the "yo-yo" syndrome which I describe later. Remember, these "back-and-forths" are most likely just temporary "fixes" and will not "fix" the real problem. Personally, I feel it is best to end the relationship by going "cold turkey," but it took me a long time of "yo-yo-ing" to get to this understanding.

Disappointment, Sadness and Depression

During this phase you will likely move into sadness. It is normal to feel sad and disappointment; after all, you've just experienced a loss. Even if you know the breakup was the right thing to do, it is still a loss of what you had wished for. You need some time to grieve your loss. While sadness is normal, depression is an extreme form of sadness, which is abnormal. Normal sadness will cause you to feel a little numb, a little off center, a little down, with a little less energy and drive, but you'll still be able to function. Depression stops you from functioning normally. Some signs of depression are loss of appetite, inability to sleep, inability to focus, inability to control your emotions, irritability, mood swings, and inability to engage in normal activities.

If your breakup was very traumatic for you and you find you are stuck in this phase, you may also be suffering from PTSD (post traumatic stress disorder). The symptoms of PTSD are similar to those with depression, and may also be complicated by acute anxiety, flashbacks, and/or nightmares. If you feel you are suffering from any of these symptoms, please get some professional help right away.

In order for wounds to heal, they need care and time. If you've ever had a serious illness or injury, you'll know you have to take care of it until it's fully healed, or it can come back and worsen. Many people stop their care when they begin to feel better, as in the common practice of stopping their medications. Any physician will tell you that you need to continue to take all your prescribed antibiotics even if you think you are all well. If you discontinue too soon, the illness or injury can come back, and this time may be more resistant to treatment. In the same way, you need to let your mind heal. This phase can take anywhere from a week to several months. If it lasts longer than several months, you need to get some professional help.

How to Get Through the Pain

People will forget what you said,
people will forget what you did,
but people will never forget how you made them feel.

--Maya Angelou

In order to heal in a healthy way, we have to go through our pain. We have to allow ourselves to really feel it. Why do we have to go deep inside our pain? Why do we have to go to that place where it hurts so much? Why can't we just take a pill or take a drink and numb it? Why can't we just replace it with a new lover?

I once had a cut on my ankle that got infected. It didn't respond to the antibiotics and kept getting worse. I had to be admitted to the hospital and have three surgeries in six days. The problem was that they had to dig into the wound and clean it out.

Not just once – not twice – but three times! They finally got it all out and it healed completely. Sometimes our mental anguish is like that. We have to go deep inside to clean out the pain – over and over. Sometimes it has to get worse before it can get better.

Yes, I know it hurts. It hurts *bad*. But as they say, what doesn't kill you makes you stronger. And this pain won't kill you! It's uncomfortable, but necessary for your full healing. I'll share with you some of the ways I've endured my pain. One way is to do your own "Gestault Therapy." Gestault believed as Freud, that there are three parts to ourselves – Our *ego* (adult), our *superego* (parent) and our *id* (child). Your child is the part that is hurting. Your parent is the part that wants to help the pain go away. Your adult is the part that is rational, objective, and mediates between the parent and the child.

Lay down and relax. First, get in touch with your child. Acknowledge its loss and pain. Allow it to cry, scream, and feel its pain. Then, get in touch with your parent. There are two types of parents – the strict, demanding parent and the nurturing, loving parent. The strict, demanding parent will tell the child she shouldn't be feeling this way and to "just get over it," as in, "just take this pill," or "you deserve better so go out and find someone new." The nurturing parent will be understanding, empathic, and caring. Be the nurturing parent and tell your child you understand her feelings. Tell her you want to make it go away, and you want her to be happy. Tell her anything you think a nurturing parent would say to a hurting child. Then, get in touch with your adult. Talk to your parent and tell her you know she means well, but your child must feel her feelings, and the best way to help the child is to allow it to hurt right now. Talk to your child and tell her you know it hurts, but it's important to allow yourself to feel your feelings fully. Tell her not to worry, because you will keep her safe. All she has to do is feel her feelings freely, and soon they will subside. Let her know that soon she will heal, and when she does, she will be able to contain even more joy. She will be stronger and smarter, and will be able to protect herself from being hurt this way again.

After a few times of doing this exercise, you will be surprised at how much better you feel. You will have acknowledged and connected the three parts of yourself. This is a skill that you will be able to use any time you have emotional distress in your life.

Another method that has helped me is to call on one, two, or three supportive people and vent my feelings with them. You'll find some of your support people aren't comfortable with your pain, and may have a tendency to become the strict parent. This is not what you need right now, so make sure you choose people who can be nurturing as well as objective for you. If they really care about you, they will be willing to listen to your venting at least a few times. You may need to keep talking about it for a while until you get it all out of you. Understand that some people may become impatient with the amount of talking and listening you need. Most people eventually become exasperated by listening to the same stories over and over. You need to also be aware of the limits of their ability to remain empathic with you, and not take it personally. If you find you have exhausted all your support people, please consider getting a professional counselor and/or attending regular 12-step meetings such as CODA.

Another method that has helped me immensely has been getting in touch with my spiritual beliefs and faith. If you have a particular spiritual path, now would be the time to allow it to help you heal and strengthen you. If you do not have one, now might be a good time to find one. Be careful however. You are in a vulnerable state. Don't allow yourself to get pulled too deeply into a new faith or religious path too quickly. Take your time, just as you would with dating a new man.

Some of the benefits of going through pain and the grieving process are:

Learning important life lessons
Experiencing pain and realizing you can overcome it
Learning coping skills
Learning self-love
Learning how to ask for support
Creating a stronger faith (in God, in yourself, in your "gut")
Learning self-protection
Gaining a stronger spirit

Acceptance

Soon you will find yourself coming out of sadness and into acceptance. This is the state Depak Chopra calls "expanded awareness." You begin to look at your situation more objectively. You begin to see solutions. You begin to see ways you can create positive change in yourself and in your life. This is the most important stage in your healing.

Sometimes we don't want to get past our sadness. In case you haven't noticed, Western society tends to focus on the negative. The media would have us all in doomsday depression if we didn't know better. Friends and relatives mean well, but sometimes they just can't help themselves. People tend to feel more comfortable in negativity and sorrow. Staying in "pain body" can become an addiction in itself.

Scientists are aware that there is a positive energy flowing through the Universe. It is this positive energy that creates life, protects life, and causes evolution and growth. This positive energy force is what causes our hearts to keep pulsing. It seems this positive energy must be <u>much more powerful</u> than negative energy, in order to sustain life. <u>It is simply a matter of which energy we choose to connect with</u>. And each moment of our lives is an opportunity for choosing – one or the other.

There are many things one can do to create and sustain the feeling of positive energy. Contrary to the old hardwired theory that the human brain is fixed from birth, the recent studies of neuroscience has revealed that our minds are reshaped through repeated experience and thought. The most important thing one can do then, to have more energy, is train their mind to focus on positivity, mainly these three aspects: acceptance, gratitude and connection.

Acceptance of what is, the way things are, the way we are, and the way others are is the basic state of mind to <u>begin</u> to unleash our positive energy. Tara Brach, a psychologist and instructor of mindfulness practice, counsels students to harness an active "yes" through something she calls <u>radical acceptance</u>. "Our basic nature is loving awareness, but we forget," Brach says. "We disconnect; we perceive separation, and along with that illusion comes most of our suffering."

An excellent means of plugging in to positive energy, is to begin with <u>self-acceptance</u>. When people are compassionate with themselves, they automatically feel better and feeling better leads to more energy. When you accept yourself (with all your baggage) you will be able to connect with your true spirit, which is the source of energy.

You can "resculpt" your own brain through relaxation, meditation, and/or prayer. Positive energy lives deep inside each of us. We need regular, consistent "mental exercise" in order to bring it forth. It's amazing that people report only spending five to ten minutes in deep, relaxed, concentrated focus can give them the same energy as if they had taken a two hour nap. When you meditate, focus on acceptance, detachment and peace. Take some time to practice and experience this state each day – it will give you positive results!

Healing

Letting go gives us freedom, and freedom is the only condition for happiness.

--Thich Nhat Hanh

With "expanded awareness" and "acceptance" comes the healing stage. This is when you will actually begin to feel better and more open to others and life in general. You will begin to feel more energy and positive lift. You may go back and forth through several stages for a while until full healing has arrived.

Social support is extremely important aspect of healing. While you may not feel like going out and socializing yet, you need to reach out to supportive people in your life. Make sure you surround yourself with people who lift you up. People are either bringing you up or bringing you down. Choose people who support, validate and encourage you.

Gratitude is another powerful mind focus. Focusing on gratitude enhances the positive connection. Something people often say, "Count your blessings," is actually a very powerful statement. Daniel Goleman, the author of *Emotional Intelligence*, discovered that the components of energy are mostly present in presence. The most energetic people he found were "lively and engaged, extremely present, involved in the moment, often funny, yet profoundly at peace – even in disturbing situations." He also said, "You always felt better than before you'd spent time with them, and this feeling lasted." One of the words used to describe this magnetic state is *sukha*, meaning "a sense of completeness, contentment, delight, calm, and abiding joy regardless of external circumstances." *Sukha* is selfless in nature and connected to a greater purpose – which is why it increases through service to others.

Reintegration

Reintegration is where you begin to feel "normal" again. Your awareness expands to others, and you are more open to new connections with people. You start to feel more confident and self-assured. You are willing to expand your social network. You desire to get outside of yourself and join more fun and interesting activities. Connection involves three components, in this order:

Connect with self
Connect with others who give and receive positive energy
Connect by serving others

Reintegration is a time of feeling empowered and exhilarated! You should commend yourself for your strength to get through this grieving process. It takes a tremendous amount of inner strength to endure and heal from a breakup. When you feel this sense of empowerment, you will be ready to begin dating again. Take it slow. Be very aware of the tendency to keep attracting the same kinds of men. Be aware and don't give your feelings away until he has proved he's worthy.

Time does heal all wounds. Time removes all "emotional charge." Trust me, it does go away! The best way to heal is to believe deeply that you deserve a comfortable relationship where you feel loved. Be aware than many men take advantage of women who don't believe they deserve more. Believe in yourself, value yourself, take care of yourself. Know that you are worthy of having a man who makes you *know and feel* you are loved.

Time is a versatile performer.
It flies, marches on, heals all wounds, runs out and will tell.

--Franklin P. Jones

Chapter Eight: How to Get Over It

I came to win
To fight
To conquer
To thrive
I came to win
Survive
Prosper
Rise
To fly

--Lines from the song *Fly* by Nicki Minaj and Rihanna

Can Chemistry Be Changed?

First of all, I don't believe there is any way to <u>increase</u> your chemistry for another person — it's either there or it isn't. It can't be forced or pushed but it can suddenly appear as if by magic. If you've just met someone new and there's no chemistry, it's unlikely it will come unless you become friends and over time this person "grows" on you. This is why it's a good idea to become friends with as many men as possible over time because you never know when one day that chemistry will suddenly appear. This happens quite a lot as women get to know men better and come to enjoy their personalities. It is especially true if this guy is fun to be around, gives you lots of positive validation, is generally a good guy, and makes you laugh. We all want to have more fun and be affirmed and validated! We may also find that this guy we once considered unattractive has become more attractive because we respect him so much. We begin to appreciate his positive traits, i.e., his stability, his dependability, his skills and talents, his ability to make us feel good and safe.

<u>Decreasing</u> your chemistry with someone you have high chemistry with is actually much easier – believe it or not! Have you ever been in a relationship where you once had high chemistry but it waned over time? Have you ever been so angry at your mate that you literally did not want him to touch you? Have you ever been so upset that this person actually disgusted you? Yes, of course you have! When a person brings us enough distress, anger and pain, we

cannot feel high sexual chemistry – it's impossible. Once I had minor surgery in two places on my body at one time. I told the doctor I only felt pain in one place – and asked him why I had no pain in the other place. He said it's because your brain can only register pain in one place at a time, so you will only feel it where it hurts most.

So if you want to decrease your chemistry with a man, you need to associate him with <u>massive doses of pain</u>. As I've said before, chemistry can decrease if this person has upset you, made you mad, or disgusted you. So what you do is think of all the ways this person has upset you, made you mad or disgusted you. You can also create a picture in your mind of that person looking very ugly or unappealing. You can also create the feeling of being disgusted, angry or strongly annoyed whenever you are with that person. What has helped me most in the past is to write a list of "all the things I didn't like about you." I wrote out a list of all his faults, all the things that bothered me, all the things he did to hurt me, and anything "bad" about him I could think of. Write your "pain" list down and read it over and over. Get an ugly picture of him and look at it over and over.

You would only want to do this of course, with someone who you honestly feel is bad for you or not right for you. We subconsciously are attracted to the same kind of people over and over, even when we KNOW this type is not good for us. You need to always be considering your highest good with all the people you hang out with. If you KNOW this person is not right or good for you, you need to move away as quickly as possible, while still keeping your dignity in tact.

I have also created an unappealing name for the person that I call him in my mind only, such as "pervert paul" or "stinky steve" or "jack the jerk." You get it. Have fun with it! Over time you will find yourself feeling less and less "turned on" and more and more "turned off!" Pretty soon, you'll be able to say, "you know I like you, but I just don't think we're a good match." That's it. It's really that easy!

Stop the Insanity!

The biggest problem women have when ending a relationship with someone they still love is <u>obsessive rumination</u>. They obsess over what happened and how they might have prevented it. They obsessively ask "Why?" They obsessively talk to their friends about it while trying to figure out why he did what he did, why he's the way he is, why he didn't love us they way we loved him, why, why, why? They need to *know*.

Well, I'm here to tell you, you DON'T need to KNOW. It doesn't matter why. He is who he is. He did what he did. He's not right for you and that's all you need to know. Ruminating won't change anything – it will only keep you wallowing in pain and misery. When you find yourself ruminating, immediately yell, "STOP" in your mind, and transfer to a positive thought. My thought is laying on the beach in Tahiti with a new man who loves me. Say to yourself over and over, "It doesn't matter, it doesn't matter, it doesn't matter." Stop the insanity!

Dating Detox

As I mentioned, it is wise not to try to replace "Mr. Wrong" with a new man, especially not "Mr. Right Now." I recommend six to twelve months of "dating detox." This is so you can heal and focus on yourself. You cannot start dating again while you are still vulnerable or you will repeat your same mistakes. You must use this time to become more empowered, more assertive, know yourself better, and create better boundaries and rules for your future self-protection.

Three Things That Will Help You Stay in Detox:

1. Have a formal name for your "program."
Patti Stanger coined the term "Dating Detox." Yours could be "Dave Detox," "Ron Rehab," "Alan Abstinence," "Larry Liberation, Narcissistic Nancy," etc.

2. Have a set time limit.
AA gives 30-day, 60-day, 90-day, 120 day, 6-month and 1 year "chips" (and more) to celebrate each time increment. One of their slogans is "One Day At a Time." It often helps to think of your detox process this way, and look forward to getting your reward or "chip" for each milestone you reach. Your minimum amount of time should be 30 days (for me it's six months). If you can't stay away

for at least 30 days you are still full on into your addiction. You cannot say you are in recovery until you have abstained for at least 30 days. The longer you were in the relationship, the longer your time limit should be. The only way to know how long it will take is to start with 30 days at a time, and at the end of each 30 days ask yourself, "When I think about him do I still have an emotional reaction?" If the answer is yes, you need more time. You need to stay in rehab until the <u>emotional charge is gone</u>.

3. Have a reward waiting for you at the end of your time limit.
Every time you think of contacting him or allowing him to contact you, you can say to yourself, "I'm in Ron Rehab for 90 days. I have only 55 days left to go, and after that I can decide what to do. I will not break this 90 day commitment to myself and my support group and I want to earn my chip!" Every time you "face down your addiction" it loses power over you.

New Commitments

You can always start over at any time, and after your time limit is up, you can choose to renew your commitment. Or you can make a new commitment. Most women find that six months to a year is enough for them to lose their addiction. Most women who thought they might be tempted to have contact after six months find that they have no desire any more.

In the meantime, take care of yourself. Here are some of the ways I've found are best for me to take care of myself:

--Get counseling or coaching
--Get into a support group
--Talk to supportive friends and family
--Go to church
--Pray and meditate
--Take baths
--Get massages, facials, manicures and pedicures
--Go to a spa
--Join a gym and go daily
--Attend CODA or Alanon meetings at least twice a week
--Read good books
--Write in your daily journal

--Go see movies (not sad or romance movies!)
--Take dancing lessons
--Take up a new sport or hobby
--Decorate your house
--Throw a dinner party
--Visit your long lost relatives
--Plan a vacation
--Take a weekend trip – even if it's alone
--Take a course or class in something you're interested in
--Start a walking group

Time does heal all wounds. Time removes all "emotional charge." Trust me, it does go away!

Throw your sticks and your stones
throw your bombs and your blows
But you're not gonna break my soul
This is the part of me
that you're never gonna take away from me.

--Lines from the song *Part of Me* by Katy Perry

Chapter Nine: Moving On and Thriving

Happiness consists of going from loss to loss without loss of enthusiasm.

--Lyn Kelley

I recommend you give it a year with no contact. It takes at least a year for permanent behavioral change. If you really want to know what might have changed with him ask him to call you in a year. Do not tell him you'll call him, and by no means should you contact him. The man is the "hunter" and he should be the one to contact you. From my experience and research, the best and most effective way to stop any addiction is to go "cold turkey." This means to STOP completely. This means NO CONTACT with the addict whatsoever, of any kind. Some women will need to get a restraining order in order to do this. If this man has threatened to harm you or your children, or has harmed you or your children, you need to get a restraining order immediately!

Self Focus

Now is the time to focus on yourself. This is not being selfish, it's being self-ful. I have found the antidote for depression is action. Even if you don't feel like it, do three things each day that you don't want to do that will improve your life. Refer back to the section about "Dating Detox." Try to stay in "Dating Detox" at least three to six months. Do not substitute another man for him. Substitute with yourself. Get some support systems in place. Reach out to friends and family. Attend CODA and/or ALANON meetings. They will be your greatest source of comfort during this difficult time.

Just think about yourself right now. Figure out what YOU really, really want. Not what others want for you, only what YOU want. This is the time – if there ever is a good time – to be self-absorbed.

What Oprah Knows for Sure About Honesty

"Ye shall know the truth, and the truth shall make you free" has always been one of my favorite Bible verses—one I memorized long before I understood what it meant. I've since learned that you can't know the truth until you're willing to know yourself—and vice versa. Knowing yourself is a lifelong process, with your biggest lessons often emerging from your biggest mistakes.

My biggest mistakes in life have all stemmed from giving my power to someone else—believing that the love others had to offer was more important than the love I had to give to myself. I did not think I was special, and that was my problem. My lack of self-respect, my belief that I needed a man to make my life all right, that was also my problem.

Then one day I got it. I recognized the truth that I am all right just as I am. I am enough all by myself.

The truth feels right and good and loving. Love doesn't hurt. Truth allows you to live every day with integrity. Everything you do and say shows the world who you really are—let it be the truth.

--Oprah, Reprinted from *O Magazine*

Since U Been Gone
I can breathe for the first time
I'm so moving on, yeah, yeah
Thanks to you, now I get, what I want
Since U Been Gone.

--Lines from the song *Since U Been Gone* by Kelly Clarkson

Chapter Ten: Comes the Dawn

      I'd like to leave you with a couple of poems I read often and have served me well. I hope they serve you well also. I hope I've comforted you, educated you, and empowered you. Please let me know if you would like relationship coaching from me to help you in the midst of a breakup. Thank you for reading this book. I want you to find real love. I want you to find real happiness. I want you to find these things in yourself, and I want you to find them in your mate. I wish you the very best relationship possible!

Let It Go
By E.E. Cummings

let it go –the
smashed word broken
open vow or
the oath cracked length
wise – let it go it
was sworn to
go

let them go – the
truthful liars and
the false fair friends
and the boths and
neithers – you must let them go they
were born
to go

let all go – the
big small middling
tall bigger really
the biggest and all
things – let all go
dear
so comes love

Comes the Dawn
By Veronica A. Shoffstall

After a while you learn
The subtle difference
Between holding a hand
And chaining a soul
And you begin to learn
That kisses aren't contracts
And presents aren't promises
And you begin to accept your defeats
With your head up
And your eyes open
With the grace of a woman
Not the grief of a child
And you learn to build
All your roads on today
Because tomorrow's ground
Is too uncertain
And futures have a way
Of falling down in mid-flight
After a while you learn
That even sunshine burns
If you get too much
So you plant your own garden
And decorate your own soul
Instead of waiting
For someone to bring you flowers
And you learn
That you really can endure
That you really are strong
That you really do have worth
And you learn and learn
With every goodbye you learn.

###

Thank You for reading this book!

By Lyn Kelley
Published by GROW Publications

Copyright 2018 Lyn Kelley

More e-Books by Lyn Kelley

Dear Jane Series:
Book 1: *The 12 Biggest Mistakes Women Make in Dating & Love Relationships*
Book 2: *How to Cure a Commitment-Phobic*
Book 3: *How to Turn a Player into a Stayer*
Book 4: *Controlling and Manipulative Men: How to Spot Them and Handle Them*
Book 5: *Self-Centered and Narcissistic Men: How to Spot Them and Handle Them*
Book 6: *Addicted Men – Drugs, Alcohol, Porn and More: How to Spot Them and Handle Them*
Book 7: *Low Achieving Men - Passives, Wimps, Dreamers: How to Spot Them and Handle Them*
Book 8: *Cheap Men: How to Spot Them and Handle Them*
Book 9: *Men who Lie and Cheat: How to Spot Them and Handle Them*
Book 10: *Emotionally Unavailable Men: How to Spot Them and Handle Them*
Book 11: *The Romantic Terrorist: Protect Yourself from Stalking, Harassment, Bullying and Threats*
Book 12: *How to Get Any Man You Want to Want YOU*
Book 13: *The 10 Biggest Mistakes Men Make in Dating & Love Relationships*
Book 14: *How to Break Up, Survive and Thrive*
Book 15: *Bad Dick, Good Jane: How Good Girls Get Bad Boys to Behave, Fall in Love and Commit*

New Release!
Bad Dick, Good Jane:
How Good Girls Get Bad Boys to Behave, Fall in Love, and Commit

Other Self-Help Books by Lyn Kelley:
How to Stick With Your Diet & Exercise Program
Light their Fire: Right and Wrong Ways to Coach and Motivate People
The 7 Self-Sabotages: Why People Sabotage Themselves and How to Stop It
How to Become Your Own Life Coach in 12 Easy Steps
How to Motivate Yourself: Secrets of the Motivational Superstars
Online Marketing for Non-Techies
The Magic of Detachment: How to Detach from Other People and Their Problems
One Day She Woke Up and Decided to Be Brave

I offer telephone and email coaching.
Contact me to set up an appointment!

lyn@janesgoodadvice.com

Follow me:
Facebook: http://facebook.com/ lyn.kelley1
Twitter: http://wefollow.com/JanesGoodAdvice
LinkedIn: http://www.linkedin.com/in/drlynisin

See my YouTube videos: Lyn Kelley

The Biggest Mistake Women Make in Dating and Love Relationships:
http://youtu.be/--aGjh3WgPc

Is He a Commitment Phobic?
http://www.youtube.com/watch?v=cLCqQHzmNOA

How to Stick With Your Diet and Exercise Program:
http://youtu.be/SEJvHJkKtSM

How to Become a Certified Professional Coach:
http://youtu.be/ZBHrDhxodWc

Bad Dick, Good Jane:
http://www.youtube.com/watch?v=QYQenwJdfW4

Learn more about Dr. Lyn and Relationship Coaching and sign up for her FREE monthly *Dear Jane Advice Column* at www.janesgoodadvice.com

Thank You!

Made in the USA
San Bernardino, CA
22 August 2019